ADVAN

"*The Relationship Train is a must for anyone that has been searching for that special someone, but has not had any luck. This book takes you on a quick, powerful and impactful journey of self-discovery and healing. Colleen Traci has done a wonderful job conveying a simple, straightforward tactic when approaching new relationships.*"

-Robert Beall

"*I just read an amazing book by an amazing Author Colleen Traci...When I began reading the book I could not stop, it was like Colleen was right here with me telling me things that feed my heart and soul. Her wisdom spread through my veins making me want to live life and fully experience The Relationship Train and Colleen Traci has been a gift to me. This is a must read*".

-Sue Gray

"As I read *The Relationship Train* I never felt alone, I felt as though the author was sitting beside me during each step of this healing journey for me. I felt as though Colleen Traci was holding my hand/ Or I was gripping her hand tightly as we went through each healing chapter of the book. It seems like she never leaves your side during this healing journey. The more I read the more healing I felt and soon I began to release the grip I had on her hand, I no longer had the need to hold her hand. Colleen Traci made me feel after reading the chapter on "Little Me" That I am important, that I matter, I have value.

Really a must read no matter where you are in life. The journey with the Author will take you on a path of knowing how to forgive yourself and others. Your will learn to accept yourself which gives you a deeper love for yourself. Then you can start to have a healthy relationship with others."

-Sherrie Stidham

"In the same way a magnifying glass amplifies, I am grateful for clear understanding as I read through The Relationship Train and all the wisdom that is in the words. I find hope in this read through practicing of self-love and healing. Letting go of my behaviors that bring me pain, I now understand how to choose healthy intentional behaviors for myself and from those I invite in my life. Having read the relationship Train has been a great gift to me."

-Melodie Knapp

The Relationship TRAIN

Be Your Own LOVE CONDUCTOR & Get a Partner Who Is on Board

COLLEEN TRACI

Difference Press

McLean, VA, USA

Copyright © Colleen Traci, 2019

Published 2019

ISBN: 978-1-68309-232-2

DISCLAIMER

Cover Design: Jennifer Stimson

Editing: Moriah Howell

Author's photo courtesy of: Boss Babe Photography

I sincerely dedicate this book to Monroe Ross Ferguson and Gloria Joan Ferguson, and to the Universe for always having my back.

TABLE OF CONTENTS

FOREWORD

Dearest reader,

If you are reading this book right now, I can say with one hundred percent accuracy that you are in, or have been in relationships in your life whether they are labeled family, friends, romantic or just super complicated... There's no escaping this very human experience of learning from each other, good or not-so-good.

The Relationship Train will provide massive insight into how to create the relationships you want, why we choose the ones we have and clarity around why past relationships have not worked out and how somehow, this experience was actually for your growth and will help you with where you want to go! This book will help you discover how you can change old patterns in order to find the true love you have been longing for. Colleen uses her intuitive work to help guide you through deep yet tangible healing exercises in every chapter.

Reading this book feels just like the sit down coffee chat I got to have with this beautiful human and I hope to warm you up and let you know first-hand about the soul behind the book you are about to indulge in and remind you, much like how Colleen came into my life, this book did not appear in your hands by chance.

I found myself sitting in a circle of mostly strangers at a retreat in a lush, beautiful and somewhat intimidating jungle. My anxiety was high for many reasons but mostly because, well, social anxiety. Forget the bugs, monkeys and bird sized grasshoppers landing in our hair. As we went around the circle one by one and introduced ourselves, I couldn't help be drawn in by the light, energy and pure joy that one woman was exuding. She introduced herself as Colleen and as she spoke I watched everyone breath a bit easier, much like how reading this book will make you feel. Her laugh was high pitched and it was one of those laughs that made you to start to laugh just by hearing it.

As the week went on I got the opportunity to spend time with Colleen and get in some very deep conversations that you wouldn't typically have (because that's what you do in the jungle with no distractions) and I found myself feeling so calm, comforted and connected to the words, the space and wisdom Colleen was sharing.

I knew this angel had floated into my life, much like a butterfly, landed on my shoulder, whispered in my ear something that shifted me and then flew off. Since then she has shown up in my life in this way offering intuitive guidance, always supporting, reminding me of my light and then she flies off to the next person who needs a blessing in their ear. That's what you will find in this book... Whispers and profound reminders of the deep wisdom inside of you that is ready to shift to a lighter, more meaningful way of life.

Colleen has a sensitive style of opening your heart as you read, that allows you to be able to feel to welcome your own healing in a very safe way while at the same time putting humor into the book to lighten things up right when you need it...

Get ready to go on a journey of unexpected healing, fun and exploration of everything you didn't know that was happening for you in your life.

Much love,
Lori Harder

INTRODUCTION

GRAND CENTRAL STATION

I n a world that is so full of people with many different diversities, ethnic cultures, religious beliefs, and different political opinions, it can be so hard to even begin finding that soulmate you have been looking for. It's as if you are getting lost in all the noise, and all that others think is right for you. We even lose track of ourselves.

It's so easy to have your vision become cloudy. Soon you start to settle because we are living in a very rushed society. It's a society where we are taught to get that college degree, find your perfect mate, have a family, and live the dream. But how do we find that partner these days to live the dream, to have that family?

Or to start over again in a new relationship? There seem to be very slim pickings of quality people that are not in a relationship already.

As you journey through this book, I want you to picture Grand Central Station. The thousands of people that are getting on and off the train. The rush off people walking, running by, the hurriedness to board the train and then the rush to get off the train. Everyone has somewhere to be, so much so that we have forgotten to look at everyone around us. Most of the time we are on our phones – maybe even trying to find that partner through social media or a dating site – or looking at the paper, or even glazed over from being in such a rush not to miss the train. By doing this, we become unengaged from those right there in front of us.

There are times when our relationships become like Grand Central Station. We get in such a rush to have a meaningful relationship that we jump into the wrong relationship too soon without looking up. Or we rush too fast to get out of the right relationship, for fear it's with the wrong partner. Either way, we are still finding ourselves single and not having that meaningful partner in our life. So, back on the train again we go. We're doing this same thing over and over again.

I think there is a better way than repeating this circle, then going through the same station day after day, doing the same things that bring you back to your original stop you started from. Maybe it's time to look at all your possibilities, and the reason why your relationships never seem to last.

I know for certain there is a perfect lover for you in this world, and I know they are waiting on you as well. I look forward to our journey together here in *The Relationship Train*.

CHAPTER ONE

HAVING THE RELATIONSHIP YOU HAVE ALWAYS WANTED

So, do you feel fed up with wasting your time on relationships that just do not work out, sick and tired of the same thing over again with different relationships, that still end up the same? Are you looking for something more, with hope of having a healthy relationship that will last this time, tired of just settling, knowing you really do deserve better? The truth is that you should be picky about who you want to spend the rest of your life with. I mean, this is your life, right? There are just so many screwed-up people out there, and you may feel as if you happen to date them all. Hmmm, ironic isn't it? Let's talk about this.

"Why?" you ask yourself. "How did I manage to find the wrong person again? I think it's time for a new dating site; I didn't like that last one anyway. Actually, that last site was the one with that creepy guy who wrote me every five minutes and kept sending me photos of his pecker, which was not that impressive anyway ... and the girl who was so needy she wanted me to move in after the second date, and when she took off her bra she went from a size D to an A and after her butt pads fall out when her pants came down, there was no butt at all. Plus, she started calling me her boyfriend on the second date. This is too much! It's all fake; none of these people seem to be who they say they are. I for sure need a new dating site. I think maybe a Christian one this time. I will find a true, real, legit nice person, but they still must be good looking."

Yes, I hear you, and I get how annoyed you must be. I have been there. It just plain sucks.

Do you feel like giving up? I'm sure you may feel at this point that relationships take too much work, and you don't have the time or energy. Finding someone to be intimate with would be great, but not worth all this effort just to have it go south again.

You're not alone. As energetic beings, we all long for companionship and love.

From the moment we are created and formed in our mother's womb, we feel a bond, we feel safe, and all our needs are taken care of. The energetic bond between mother and child creates one of love, the two are one as the child is forming. Then the miraculous day comes of the child being born, the cord is cut, and what was once one in the womb has now become two.

This very moment in our life starts the desire and the need for companionship, for we were not created to do life solo, but to join together with love.

When a baby cries, they have needs to be met. They may be hungry, need their diaper changed, or just feel a desire to be held and comforted. Nevertheless, a need to be met. Here in this nurturing stage is where we start to feel emotions. Love is the highest of these emotions, and from this time forward you will find yourself seeking love. Still, a baby does not yet understand all the different kinds of love there are. But they know instinctually that it involves them and another source. This is where your intuitive energetic being knows you need companionship.

We grow into our adult forms longing and seeking love, friendship, and partners, for we do not want to feel alone. We take with us all that we have learned from infancy to childhood into our adulthood. We do exactly what we think we should be doing, with the knowledge we have learned along the way to our present state of mind.

Relax – you are not going to grow old and alone. There is no need for that, because that special person is also searching for you as you read this book. You are now being prepared and shaped for the love of your life. You may have to do some shifting and navigating through this adventure of finding your perfect partner, the one who gets you, who understands you, who puts you as a priority in their life. Just know you are both preparing to meet each other right now, and your day of connection is coming.

Everyone you come in contact with is no accident, as each and every person has been brought to you divinely. Even the horrible ex who you hate and can't even understand why you were with someone like that. Yep, I just said what you thought I said. I will say it again: each and every person has been brought to you divinely. Did that sound better the second time? I'm guessing not, and why should it? It's not your fault you're a magnet for crappy relationships.

I have good news! Prepare for the right relationship, the right partner, because he or she is about to come your way. As we move forward in learning how to find that dynamic relationship you long for, your eyes will begin to open your mind to new ideas, thoughts, and discoveries.

Let's keep moving on and forward, because there's no need to look back at the past. Those relationships are done and did not serve you, so why look back? Don't let your past bad relationships affect the possibilities of the new one to come. We can't hold someone else hostage to what another has done wrong to us. We can only grow and learn from those hurts. I say, do you want to be better, or bitter? How about better, so that way you find your soulmate?

Deal? Good.

CHAPTER TWO

MY STORY

I remember the first time I said, "I do." I was just eighteen years old, just a young girl thinking she knew what she was doing. And, really, I would not have listened to anyone anyway. I knew I was in love, but still I felt numb, and a little lost in all the craziness of planning a wedding in thirty days. Thank God my mother-in- law-to-be took the reins and made that day happy and beautiful. See, on my wedding day I was three months pregnant, and I didn't want to show that I was pregnant. After all, I had to look gorgeous in my white dress, acting as if I was some kind of Virgin Mary, all in white, not yet showing. I married a man I had only known for five months and did so thinking,

"Yes, this is going to be the perfect marriage." That was the day I started living a false reality. I had no idea that I was creating any kind of false reality. That hadn't even occurred to me.

About six months later, I gave birth to an adorable baby boy. Life was amazing except for the fact that my husband and I could not get along. I became pregnant with our second child. We were already arguing all the time and about to have two children fifteen months apart – that created so much more tension and anger towards one another. Time went by and we had our second boy, who was so cute and brought happiness into our lives. But we were not happy with each other. We were being horrific to one another, there were very few days that went by that we did not call each other horrible names.

We both were working; my husband worked during the day and I worked for a department store at night. We had decided we didn't want to have our children in daycare, so we worked opposite shifts. Take not seeing each other hardly at all combined with when we did see each we were tired and trying to survive life's struggles.

So, we would fight instead of joining together. This became our normal. It was all becoming too much.

I realized at this point that I had created a false reality with a man I hardly knew and who hardly knew me. In my mind, he was the perfect man for me, and I was so lucky to have met him and be his wife. I kept thinking, "Maybe tomorrow will be different," and "If I just try harder...." But every day was the same – more and more fighting, or not talking. My dream come true ... *not!* I was very unhappy, lonely, and felt very unloved, undesired, ugly, and as though I had no meaning. I felt as though he never saw me and really could care less if I was around. I became even more unsure than the day I met him. And, of course, I would feel even worse because he was telling me these things on a consistent basis. I also told myself these same things. I was also yelling and calling him horrible names. Neither one of us were innocent.

Around this time was when I started enjoying the attention from my boss. Yes, flirting with danger, but it felt so good to have that attention. My husband and I ended up separating when our sons were three and four. I didn't think we would get back together, even though we were seeing a therapist to work on things. I didn't have any hope.

The excitement and flirting with my boss were growing more intense. Yes, that night came when I gave into all my desires and fantasies, and I had sex with my boss. Afterward, I felt horrible, empty, and so unfulfilled. And still I didn't feel loved – I was just as insecure as I was before I slept with him. I ended that fling immediately.

After a time, my husband and I got back together. We both really wanted to do the right thing for our children, so we gave it another shot. I had had a one-night affair with my boss, which I honestly didn't feel that guilty at all, and that bothered me more than the act itself. "Colleen, you should feel bad. It's weird that you don't. Do you really love your husband?" I asked myself this question many times. But I really did want to try in my marriage. I didn't want to be like my parents, who both had been married over three times. I didn't want my boys to have a divided family or have them go through the hurt of what divorce can do.

For this reason, I kept thinking, "Of course I am committed to him – that's love."

Then guess what happened. You got it; I became pregnant with our third child. Of course, a baby brought so much light into our lives, but it still did not really change us as a couple. Yes, we were kinder to each other for a short period of time. We were as kind as two people could be who didn't know how to love, give, or care for another person in a positive way. We were doing the best we knew how to do at this time in our life.

We separated three times during our marriage, till the day came when I said, "I am done. I've had enough of this dysfunctional nightmare we put each other through almost every day." We would go to church fighting but walk through the church doors acting as though we were happy. We were teaching our boys all the wrong things, the wrong feelings, the wrong emotions, the wrong way to treat the person you are supposed to love the most. That was it; it had to stop. This took twenty years to say and do with certainty. Two of our boys were in high school the other going into junior high. I had hoped to make it till they had all graduated from high school, but I just could not live a lie and in turmoil any longer. There just had to be a better way.

I won't get into the faults or the details of what took place in our marriage or during our divorce, for that will serve no one in this book, you the reader, or my past. I will say that for a time, things got very ugly and a lot of hurt was done, to each other and to our children.

I thought, "That's it! I never want to be with a man again. Twenty years of feeling unwanted, unloved, unheard ... I'm not doing this again. I am done with relationships and men."

At this time in my life, I was working in the banking industry. I was actually feeling pretty happy and relieved to have left my husband. It made me feel very independent and that felt *so* good! It gave me so much strength and hope.

I had become good friends with my co-workers and was really enjoying the time we would spend after work having wine and talking. But there was one woman I really started becoming close to. In fact, I thought of her almost every night after leaving work. We started flirting with each other. This was very unexpected to me, but still I was enjoying it.

We started seeing each other, and for about nine months on and off we both were just trying to figure who we were and what we wanted. But I was having fun being together, even as dysfunctional as it was. I wasn't seeing the dysfunction at that point. Just that the relationship was something very different and felt right to explore whatever it was that we were doing.

I'm still didn't want anything to do with men. For some reason, I thought it would be different having a relationship with a woman, that a relationship with a woman would be easier than with a man. For sure I thought it would be much kinder. This is not the case. It was still hard, and we would fight. I realized that relationship was not what I wanted. I wasn't even sure if we could say that what we were doing with one another was a relationship. The only thing I knew for sure is this was not working for either one of us.

One day, an incredibly hot guy came in the bank.

Of course, I knew that I was going to date him – it was just the way we looked at each other, and my intuitive side was on high alert. *Warning: not the guy you should be dating.* Yep, I ignored that voice. The connection was strong, and we were having a blast together. That is, until the day his girlfriend walked in and found us in his bed together. I obviously didn't know he *had* a girlfriend! It was not the movie scene I wanted to be in. Luckily, I never really shared with anyone about my time with him. My spirit warned me to be careful in introducing him to my children and some of my friends.

I started dating, and none of the men really impressed me. I was pretty much bored, and I just knew there was something/someone with so much more for me. Then, a man walked up to my desk at the bank and said he needed some help with his account. We started talking, and soon both realized we were each going through a divorce. This man was different. I felt a connection, but a much deeper connection than on the surface. "Hmmm," I thought to myself, "this is a super nice guy. I should have him over for Easter and introduce him to my friend." God forbid I should think of dating the nice guy! We had a great time on Easter together. He asked me out on a date, but I said, "No, I'm a mess and I would just hurt you. But here, meet my friend." I'm so happy they didn't end up dating!

I realized that all this dating was getting me nowhere, and I couldn't seem to find that right man or woman. I started seeing some huge patterns in myself. I knew I needed to do something about my destructive behavior. I was just hurting myself; I needed to fix my man-picker that was my problem! Well, not quite. I had to take a good look at myself and do some self-repair. It took a year to discover *me*: all the things I liked about me and all the things I needed to improve with myself. This was a very enlightened path for me.

I was still friends with the nice man from the bank. I decided to call him and tell him I would like to date him. The dating journey has now brought us to nine years of marriage! Terry is my lover and my best friend ... but I had to discover me before him and I could ever be.

CHAPTER THREE

HAPPY NEWS – THERE IS A SOLUTION TO THIS PROBLEM

The solution to this problem is a lot simpler than you think. It truly is learning how to be your own conductor. For so much of our lives we are told what to do, what to think, and even how we should feel. We forget in our adult years that it's really our choice what relationships we choose to have or not to have. The truth is that you are your very own conductor; you are very capable of making the right decisions for yourself in finding a partner who is ready to jump on board with and play full-out in life and love with you. You just need to clear your vision, so you know the clear path you are looking or heading toward.

Get rid of all past relationships from your mind. The good, the bad ... whatever the case may be. You can't move forward if you are still living with a past partner in your mind. No one will even have a chance of being able to be seen by you for who they are if you're holding someone else in your thoughts. So, setting your conscious to a free, clear state is very important, so that you can be open to receiving that perfect partner for yourself. Of course, you want to make sure you pick the partner who is right for you and who gives you the love and kindness you deserve. That's why it's even more important to release past lovers from your thoughts. I'm sure you don't want to make the same mistake by having that type of partner again in your life, the one you are no longer with because of the way they mistreated you. So, the great news is that you get to be your very own conductor in all areas of your life, especially when it comes to having the mate you long for. If you're wanting to find that forever partner, then you for sure want to be the one conducting your relationships!

Life and people pleasing can be distractions from following our hearts' true desires. As we travel through this book, my goal is to help show you how you can meet your partner, the one who meets your heart's desire, and not allow yourself to settle for anything less. You do deserve the best. So, in these next seven chapters we will explore your options, give you new ideas of ways to meet that person for you. You will be given tools that help you, and techniques to help guide you on your path.

We will look at patterns that no longer serve you in finding your soulmate. These steps you will find useful in all your relationships, including:

- Co-workers
- Family members
- Friends
- But most of all finding your perfect love

What we are going to do is bring clarity to the situation. You have dealt with enough cloudiness, so let's get things brighter through clear understanding of the path you have been on to the new path you will begin. These chapters will help enlighten you and give you clear steps that should be taken to bring forth your intention to find true love.

As we go through our journey, there will be times when self-critical chatter will come in and have you doubt yourself. Things like, "It must be my fault that something must be wrong with me," or all the concerns of "I'm not good enough.... Why would anyone want to date me?" There's so much self-blaming that this self-critical chatter is all we hear. Please know that these words are just wreaking havoc on your mind and creating hardship in your life.

So, as we take this journey, let's be aware of when self-critical chatter starts to eat away at you, so that you don't allow any self-doubt to stop your progress. This way you can stay open to receive all the magic that awaits you during this book journey.

We are going to have some funny times on this journey, but we will also be serious. Maybe even tears will come as you begin to allow yourself to be vulnerable and awaken in awareness. You will start to see things very clearly, and your lenses of how you have been seeing relationships will change with new vibrant colors. You will experience a spiritual awaking as your consciousness grows deeper into an enlightened space.

We will take this journey together, so know that you are not alone. I'm here all the way through this transformational experience with you.

Remember, be light and don't take yourself too seriously as we go through this journey. We are all here in human form having a spiritual experience. So, please don't be hard on yourself. Let's make a pact. Sounds good? Great! Let's try to allow love, acceptance, and forgiveness to be our tour guides as we journey forth in *The Relationship Train*. The outcome is one that I am sure you will be grateful for. It was a life-changer for me!

CHAPTER FOUR

ABANDONMENT AND BEING LEFT BEHIND

He left without a word, leaving an infant never to
know him. She, because of him, raised me hard.
I was left with a strong woman for a mother,
for now we both were abandoned, and left behind.
My mother's life goal was not to love me,
but to make me strong, to make me stronger
than she ever was. I was not to feel the pain of
abandonment, but just to be strong.

ANONYMOUS

Here is where it all starts. Yes: in this very
moment our walls come up, and our protective
defenses are in play. Rejection (*ouch*) from the people
who should love us the most, our parents.

You may think things like, "If they can leave me and they are my parents and they say they love me, then why wouldn't everyone else in my life leave me, even though they also say that they love me? Love equals leaving. I am not important, I really don't matter. Why try? In time they will leave, too. They will leave just like everyone else, and I will have to be alone and strong. I can only depend on myself. This is what you know to be true, because it is what has happened to you as a child."

Having fear of abandonment leaves you with huge insecurity issues. This is where insecurities bind to your psyche (the human soul, mind, or spirit). These insecurities do not show themselves in a direct manner. They actually hide from us, then creep up on us when we least expect it. Yes, we may know we are insecure about our weight, maybe our skin, our hair, how we appear on the outside. We may know our insecurities from our outward appearance, but do not realize insecurities from the inner space from deep within us.

Remember they hide deep in our soul, mind, and spirit, (the psyche) so they can be hard to recognize.

Here are some clues when you're acting out of insecurities in your relationships of things you might say:

- Okay, I'm not good enough for you
- I don't need you
- You think I'm dumb
- I'm not dumb
- So, you think I'm ugly
- I know you don't love me
- You're just using me
- Are you cheating on me?
- I know you're cheating on me
- Why are you not picking up my call?
- You are ten minutes late; why are you not home yet?
- Forget this, I'm out of here
- I don't need you
- You think you're better than me
- You're not better than me

Any of those statements ever come out of your mouth? Are you laughing just a little at the fact that you have said some of the same words? You might be thinking, "Those words have come out of my mouth, and much more!" Those are just some of the statements we say in moments when insecurity is creeping out of us, rearing its ugly head. The words come out as a form of protection for yourself. Those words feel very real, and you will believe them to be true because how you feel seems so real. But insecurity is sneaky, and it lies to you. It will feed you falsehoods about who you are and how you see others perceiving you.

This was planted in you from the very moment of abandonment. No, you did not cause this at all. It was not your fault that you were ever abandoned as a child. You were born into a world innocent, you were a baby, a child, a teenager. Abandonment should have been something you never went through or felt. I am very sorry you have had to feel this deep pain.

When you feel abandoned, you put up walls of protection, for you can't trust anyone. You know that eventually they are going to hurt you, and you are right – they will. You make sure they do.

"Okay, Colleen, what are you talking about? I don't make people hurt me, they just do. I'm a nice person, they're the jerk/horrible person that did this to me."

I hear you! Don't throw the book away and stay with me on this. Just keep reading and you may begin to understand why you could be a part of the reason you keep getting hurt. Remember, I am right here on this journey with you. So please don't feel your alone.

In this place where we have put up walls of protection, we have made it impossible to have deep, meaningful relationships. See, a person can only get so far into your heart. Let's just say our heart is the place where we carry love, and we accept love and give love. When this person starts to penetrate your heart and you start feeling real emotions of love, you will start sabotaging the relationship, though not intentionally. This is your psyche protecting you or giving you a falsehood of protection. You want the relationship, you really do. But that Little You who's hurt does not want you to let your walls down. We will talk more about Little You in Chapter Seven.

Subconsciously you might be thinking, "No, no, they can't; this will hurt again. Stop, close off, feel insecure, it's *safer*. Come on, say some mean words. Hurry! They're getting close. Yes, good job, I convinced you to sabotage the relationship. That was a close one this time!" This happens so fast we do not even realize where it came from, just that our feelings are very real. Then we start the blame game: "They were so selfish; what a jerk; what a witch." On and on and on. You're not lying when you say that stuff, because you believe it. You know you're right, that's all there is to it.

But really there is so much more to this. All these hurts were placed there as a child; it is what always has been for you. It does not even seem dysfunctional to you. Oh, but I bet you see the person you broke up with as dysfunctional. Of course you do! You would only attract someone dysfunctional – odds are against you picking a healthy partner, because you're still needing to heal. That's okay, though, because you are on the right path now, and you are going to finally learn and see more about you and your relationships so that you can have that beautiful relationship you so desire. I know this is hard, but it's the good stuff truly, and, in the end, you will be so happy we took this book journey together.

Take a deep breath, unwind, stretch, go to the restroom, go get a glass of water. I will be right here waiting for you.

You're back! Good. Let's keep moving full steam ahead. Now, I do want to add that it is very possible that you really do end up in a relationship with that jerk or witch. Call them whatever name you would like. You attract that type of person, so it could end up really being the other person's stuff that ends your relationship. Again, I bet they do not even realize they're doing the same things you have done. Now, this is where you have to really look at this. It's still you, you still picked a relationship that would not work no matter who ends up ending it. You will discover more about this process as we move along.

There is another side to abandonment I feel we should talk about.

You may pick the wrong partner and stay with them out of fear of being left, giving you that feeling of abandonment all over again. You could stay with this partner for years because of the fear of abandonment.

You will allow this partner to do things that are not kind to you, say things that are cruel to you, while all along you are doing everything you can to please your partner. It will never be enough for this partner; most likely you picked a partner who is very controlling.

Why did you pick this partner? "Because they seemed like they had it all together!" This is common – you think they would be safe and take care of you, that they would bring back the safety you lost when you were abandoned. It's a perfect portrait for someone dealing with abandonment problems. This partner may even control you by telling you they are going to leave you, if you do not comply to their demands. So, you beg them not to leave and you comply.

This has you lost inside. It has you feeling even more insecure that they could leave you at any moment. You will probably have a lot of anxiety and depression in this type of relationship, and you will try to hide this from your partner for fear of upsetting them and not wanting them to leave you. In time, this will physically take a toll on your body and you can become ill. I bring this up because it's important for you to recognize this and for you to understand. This type of a relationship is a very dangerous one. This partner can be very harmful to you and is not a safe partner for you to be with.

I really would like you to look at this section and make sure you are not living in fear of being alone. If you are, please know you do not have to live in or stay in fear. You have all the strength inside of you to live alone but not be alone. You have made it this far in your life and survived, I know you can make the best decision for yourself by loving yourself enough to break free from this type of destructive relationship. You do matter. And the right, most loving partner is out there waiting for you. *You got this!*

Abandonment stinks big time. It leaves you to deal with the hurt that was planted in you by someone else. Good news is that you're dealing with it now, you already started the healing.

"I'm healing, you say?" Yep, you are! You almost made it to Chapter Five! Be proud of this, even though there's still a way's to go.

At this point, you still may have some worry and may not see a love in sight. Or maybe you think you're not lovable. This is *not true!* Your thoughts are normal. You're still healing – don't forget that you're in the beginning stage of healing. You're seeing things a little differently now in this chapter. You may even have some anger right now. Good! Feel that, keep leveled but allow yourself to feel your different emotions. Feeling is good. You have been in a shell for a long time, and it will take some time for your shell to completely open. You really do matter, and you are very important to this world or you would have never been brought into it. You are lovable. You deserve to love yourself first and foremost and you can have the love of your life at the same time.

CHAPTER FIVE

LOSS OF INNOCENCE

Do you recall the first time your heart was broken?
I was sitting on my bunkbed in the room I shared
with my two sisters. Only on this day it was just my
little sister and I in the room. Our door opens
and it's our father.

"Well your mother left me for another man, she met
him at work over the phone."

He said this so plainly. We knew something had
been wrong, since our mom before the last few
months never drank alcohol or smoked, never
cursed, never even dressed close to provocative
and now she is like a completely different person.
Overnight the mother we knew was gone.
Our perfect family was not perfect any longer.
You don't wish for this to happen, you may not even

see this coming. But in a moment in time such as this you will never forget. When your happiness is taken from you and not by choice. It's a loss; a loss of innocence.

HALEE KOBERLEIN

If only we lived in a perfect world where we as children do not have to endure the pain of losing our innocence based on the choices others have made for our innocent lives. But that is just not the case.

Abuse in our childhood is something that we don't like to talk about. It's actually most likely from having it told to you as a child that you're not to talk about what happened in your home, or that you have taken on so much shame that isn't yours to own. You have held this pain from your childhood in your psyche for years, masking your pain. By doing this you may start to live a type of lifestyle to cover up that shame and the pain. This may be a lifestyle that is distractive to you. It will happen unintentionally; you may not even see it. You may find yourself consuming large amounts of alcohol or even using drugs to numb this pain that happened so long ago. Oh, it may be fun for a while, but I'm guessing if you're reading this and we are taking this journey together, you're tired of hurting and repeating the same patterns. You may also be seeing this lifestyle has not led you to finding the right partner.

Now, it may not start out as a problem, but when it becomes your crutch or a replacement for an emotion or a person missing in your life or a way of hiding from your pain, then it will be become a huge issue for you if left undealt with. I tell you this so that you look at the entire picture as we journey together. This does not make you bad or wrong in who you are as a person. It doesn't make you an alcoholic, or a drug addict. It just makes you a human, who may have to deal with healing. Please remember we all have our stuff, and how I know this is because I have ventured in these areas. Let's still give grace to ourselves as we keep going on this journey.

Sex is great, and it is even more amazing with someone you love. But when you go looking for sex to feel loved and to fill a void that you lost long ago, it will always leave you feeling empty. You can't make love to someone you just met, you're just plain having sex with someone you just met. That will not fill the void in you; it will only create a larger hole. You may feel good that day/night or even for a week or two, but your crash will happen, taking you deeper in the hole. Yes, physical connection is intense, and that sexual passion is fun and feels good, but what happens when that wears off? What are you left with? Sex does not equal love. It's just a fun part of being in love.

When you lose your innocence at a young age, you tend to look for love through sexual experiences, feeling as though this will validate you as being important to someone who does not even know you. This is why it's important to feel your loss from your childhood. Because you can have both: Your perfect love and making love to your lover.

First, let's get you out of that hole. Guess what? I have a rope – it's this book. By reading it, you're helping yourself out of the hole. That's awesome! I'm here with you all the way, so don't worry about falling into any more holes.

Depression can be a part of loss of innocence. When you long to have that childhood back, the one before everything fell apart, it holds you in a place of the age where everything fell apart. You are stuck in that age in your psyche. Remember this from Chapter Four? Without knowing it, you become depressed, longing for something that can never be again. It's the past and it can't be fixed. It happened.

But it can be healed. I can remember what it felt like to be depressed. Wanting to stay in bed, not wanting to see anyone, thinking no one understood what I was going through, actually feeling sick. Depression certainly did not help me in any relationship. I had to break free from it. I could not stay in that state, it would kill me for sure. So, accepting the things I could not change and feeling the pain was my only option at that point. It was a great option! Because I so wanted to live and live happily and be in love. I wanted to laugh with my lover, cuddle with my lover, cry with my lover. I desired the good stuff that was taken when I lost my innocence.

It was not too late! I realized I could create a new space for myself; *I* could become new. The loss of my innocence would not matter because I was new. I let the old me go and started a new clear path for the new me to journey on.

You too can become new and have all the good stuff you dream about. It's all here for you. You can do this!

What have we learned here in our loss of innocence that does not serve us?

1. We grow up way too fast
2. We start destructive behaviors to cover our loss
3. Hiding from our abuse takes us deeper in a hole
4. Depression can be a part of not dealing with our loss

I am so happy and proud of you. We just walked together through a very tough chapter. It may have been hard, but you did it. This is so good, and it's going to get even better as we move forward. I know you have all kinds of thoughts and emotions – that's okay! You should; this is a process. It's the end result we want the most.

CHAPTER SIX

BECOMING A VICTIM TO YOURSELF

I can remember at such a young age hearing my mother complain. I don't even recall a day when she didn't complain. There was always something wrong, or someone to talk about. I remember her talking about my Uncle Tom and his wife and how they always did our family wrong. I remember her speaking about my father and how she did everything for him and he did nothing, that without her everything would fall apart. Her words were, "After everything I have done for you, this is how you act, this is what I get. It's never enough. I will never be enough; I should just die, then you would miss me and see everything I do."

ANONYMOUS

It's so easy to fall into repeating patterns in our lives. You watch and listen to someone for eighteen years, so it's easy to be somewhat like them. Even if you say to yourself, "I will never be like my mother or my father." *Ha!* Yeah right! It just happens. Before you know it, you're saying, "I just sounded like my mom" or "That is something my dad would have done." Sometimes we can even become a victim like one of our parents.

When we do not have healthy love for ourselves, we can become a victim. This is a scary place to be because we can pick a partner that may be physically, mentally, and even emotionally abusive to us. If we cannot see our value, then why would we pick a partner that would see our value?

When you're in victim-mode, it's an easy excuse to allow people to mistreat you and to not deal with the lack of love you have for yourself. You can just complain about how you're treated, but you don't do anything. So, they keep mistreating you until you decide not to be a victim any longer.

How you decide that is simple. You may think and say it's not simple, because being a victim has worked for you all these years, but it really is simple. Now, I am not saying it won't hurt, when you set guidelines for your loved ones on what you are and are not willing to allow in your life. You may find your friends and family get upset at you for setting guidelines. You may even have to say good-bye to some of the people in your life for now. Yes, your loved ones will be angry because they can't treat you like crap any longer or take advantage of you. For sure this is going to upset some people in your life. But they will get over it, and those who don't – well, do you really want those people in your life? That's something for you to think on.

I want you to close your eyes and imagine yourself in your happiest state of mind. Imagine who you are with. It may be no one, because right now there could be no one who makes you happy, and that's okay. Completely feel where you are at right now.

Now, let's go to a deserted island. You are there by yourself; no one else around. You are sitting and thinking about your life, where you are and how you got here to this point of feeling alone and lonely. Okay, so now with that thought in the back of your mind, close your eyes. You are still on this deserted island, just with yourself, except I want you to envision you completely in love with yourself. You are proud of who you are and how far you have come from the person you once were. You are whole; you are at peace with you. And you see all the beauty you are and all the light you bring to the world. You are amazing, and you love yourself. You see your value, there is no one like you in the world. You are uniquely made, and that makes you priceless and so very valuable. Okay, open your eyes. What thoughts did you find brought you more happiness? Write it down now. I want you to put this answer in an envelope or folded in a safe private place for only you to see. We will be opening this at some point during our book journey

How are you doing? You may want to try and journal that thought on how you're doing and what you're feeling. If you don't like to journal, then just take time to process.

CHAPTER SEVEN

LITTLE ME

We all have our inner child that lives in us. What this child's childhood was like will be the deciding factor on where this child will plant its seeds in our being. In a perfect world seeds will be planted in our heart – remember this from Chapter Five? The heart is the carrier of love. But let's face it; it's not a perfect world. Nor would I want it to be! I enjoy imperfectness. It's in our flaws that we find impeccable beauty. So, in this not-a-perfect world, your not-so-perfect childhood is where the Little Me would most likely plant their seeds in your psyche. Your conscious mind does not even now this Little Me is living in you. Let's just call Little Me a she in these next two chapters. But remember, if you're a man reading this insert 'he' in your brain as you read. Little Me does not discriminate; this applies to you in the same way.

When traumatic events happen to you as a child, this Little Me has to find a safe place to go, a place where they can hide and feel protected. She started hiding long ago during the times these events took place. You will find there to be many different ages. So the Little Me may have lots of ages that have to be released.

Example:

When I was three, my sister (who was eight at the time) and I walked to the corner gas station to get candy. Who knows where my parents were. While we were there, the gas station was held up at gun point. We were locked in the bathroom for over an hour. Now, I don't remember this event. I have been told about it, and told I screamed the entire time, and that my sister was told to "shut me up" or they would kill us. My poor sister, only eight, dealing with me, who was kind of a brat.

Then I was about twenty-two, my two boys (who were four and three) were with me at the laundromat. We were the only ones there. I had to use the restroom, so we all went in and I locked the dead bolt behind me. When we tried to leave, I went to turn the lock, and it would not turn. I thought, "Crap it's not working!" My heart started pounding, faster and faster. I got dizzy. *No!* We were locked in the bathroom and there was no one there. *Help, help!* I remember my two boys were watching this and how I reacted.

I started screaming louder and louder. I banged on the door, and my two boys started to join in on my panic. They were screaming and banging on the door with me. I thought, "We are never getting out of this bathroom!" I started crying, and my breathing got very heavy. I had a full panic attack. My poor boys started crying. Of course they were taking on my emotions. My boys were probably thinking, "You're the parent, so you must know what we should do!" Not the case; I was in complete panic.

This went on for twenty minutes. I said to myself, "Stop, Colleen, this is not helping. Think what it is doing to your boys." I calmed down somewhat. We were sitting on the ground in this dirty bathroom for three hours. Worn out, we all started to fall asleep. Then, we heard a man's voice! We all three jumped up and started yelling and banging on the door. Finally, with the help of some tools, this man got us out. Little Me came out full force; she was buried so deep I did not know she was there.

Claustrophobia at its finest, put there when I was just three. I have since healed that three-year-old and released her, for she did not serve me anymore. I'm no longer afraid to lock bathroom doors, or any doors, from inside with me in the room. I can go into elevators and small confined spaces. I am no longer a hostage to the three-year-old Little Me.

Another Example:

When I was nine, my mother tried to kill herself with a blade to her wrist. I was the only one home and I had to stop her. We struggled. I finally got the blade away from her and wrapped up both her wrists with washcloths, trying to stop the bleeding. I ran to my neighbor for help. I didn't even notice the cuts on myself from the struggle until after the ambulance got to our home, and the paramedic cleaned and bandaged my cuts. My mom lived but spent a couple of days in the hospital. From that day on I could not hold a blade.

Then, eight years ago my husband said, "Can you hand me that blade on the counter?"

I froze, thinking, "I can't." I heard a voice say, "Don't do it."

But I did, and sure enough I ended up slicing my thumb open. There came the blood. I ran to be by myself in the bathroom. I could not have him see me, because the tears started pouring from me. I saw that day all over again. I needed to hide. I had to get this blood cleaned up, so I could move past this, as if that was my cure.

My husband asked, "What was that about and why would you not let me in?"

My response? "I didn't want to worry you with me bleeding, so I cleaned it up before you saw it."

I knew it was time for me to get over the fear of blades and blood (that sounds like a good movie title). It's not like the blade was going to chase me and cut my wrist! But that Little Me sure wanted to keep me afraid of the blade.

About six months ago, I was planting flowers and putting soil into the pots. What do I grab? You got it – I grabbed a blade. I took the blade and put it up, calm as could be, not afraid at all and then cleaned my cut. I had healed the Little Me from age nine and that event with my mom. See, eight years ago when my husband asked for the blade, I cried for over two hours. Then I said, "Little nine-year-old Me, you have to go. You cannot hold me hostage to this hurt any longer. I love you, but it's time for you to go." I released her from my psyche and I healed from that event.

With those two examples, I hope I can lead you into understanding how important it is to release the Little You and release all the different ages. One by one. Going through all your different ages from as far back as you can remember or from what you have been told.

She may not have been hurt just from family. It could be from a bully at school, from being hurt by a friend, a teacher, or even a stranger. All different people and different ways. The thing is she needs to be healed and released at each age that this hurt took place. Once you do that you are free to be lighter, happier, and healthier.

Little Me is not trying to hurt you. She is just keeping herself locked away till something happens and she shows up. You're probably wondering, "Where the hell did that reaction come from!?" and "Why did I just act that way?" You can't even explain it, because you don't even know it's you as a child in your adult form.

You will find as she comes out when you're triggered that a lot of the time it displays as anger. It can be something small, but that was huge to that little child and it comes out ugly. No, you don't need a priest, or an exorcism (unless your head starts spinning and does a 360). I know you do not want to react out of anger because it takes so much energy. I know you just want happiness and peace. So, let's get that for you. Happiness and peace are the best ways to feel!

How can it be that you have yourself holding you hostage? This Little Me has been there so long that she has never negotiated with you for your release. You been doing just fine, Little You and Adult You. Why would she want to free you?

Imagine a life with deep intimate connections, a life where you love yourself and all that you are, a life where you have a happy, flourishing relationship. A home built in love and peace. This dream is a reality that you can have. So, time to say, "Good-bye, Little Me! You cannot hold me hostage any longer. I love you, but you are not allowed to live here in me any longer! The adult me needs to be loved now."

Maybe we should get up and stretch. While you're at it, grab a pen, paper, a mirror, and some tissues. We are going to do an exercise on releasing this Little Me.

Alrighty, that stretch felt good. How are you doing? Well, remember this is all a process, and just think of your outcome. Know I am right here with you and you're not alone. Are you ready? Good, let's do this! You will want to be alone, just you and I, during this exercise.

Close your eyes. I want you to think of the first childhood memory you have of trauma, hurt, disappointment, sadness, being picked on, etc. There is no wrong answer. Go with the first one that comes in your head. There, right there! Write that down. Good.

Now, put the age you can remember this taking place next to your answer, get close, it does not have to be the exact age next to the answer you put. Can you please pick up the mirror and hold it in front of your face?

I'm going to give you an example of what you should say: "Seven-year-old Little Me, I love you. You matter. I am so sorry you were hurt. But you can't stay here any longer. I have to move forward in my life, and, Seven-year-old Me, you do not serve me. I love you. Good-bye."

Now, keep on writing times you remember hurt and the age it happened. Do this process with each one. You may have twenty, you may ten, you may have eight, you may have one. Whatever the number is it's okay. Just do the example with each one. You may feel tears coming up as you release Little Me. That's okay – let them come out, pour out if need be. If you have a knot in your throat that really hurts, that would be you holding back tears, so let them come out. You're safe; it's just us here.

Little You is going to try to stop you from doing this. A distraction may come, or you will start to feel an emptiness come on, or even a sadness for letting them go. Those are okay to feel, but keep on saying good-bye to Little Me just like the example says.

Remember I said I would tell you a little more of my story later in the book? Well, it's later.

I grew up in Southern California. I'm the youngest of seven children. We were a blended family, so three of my brothers and one sister grew up in a different home with their mother. My other brother and sister and I all grew up together. I went to six elementary, one junior high, and four high schools. Both my parents were alcoholics, and my mom was also addicted to prescription medication. There were not many times in my life that I can account for them being sober.

My father was very abusive when he drank, especially to my mom. I can say he really didn't abuse me, not like he did my other siblings, and for sure not like he did my mom. My mom was a very sad woman who tried to kill herself three times. Looking back, she was slowly trying with the drugs and alcohol as well. When I was fifteen my mom finally succeeded: she had drunk so much alcohol and had taken enough pills to become incoherent. She fell and hit her head, and her brain bled to death. The autopsy report had said cirrhosis of the liver as well. Either way, she passed.

So, there is a short version of part of my life. I, too, did the Little Me steps with myself. It changed my life; changed my story. I love my parents! They really did the best they knew how. I forgive them completely. Because of that, I can move past those hurts through my forgiveness. And I can see them as their own hurt Little Me's, who never had any help becoming whole. I don't want to go into everything in great detail, for this book and journey we are doing together is for you to heal. I'm telling you the short version, so you know

I get the pain of Little Me and how I had to do this healing method as well.

Wow. This was an intense chapter, I know. Great job – I know for sure that was not easy, because I have also done this work before. You did it! This is a transformational moment – take some time to celebrate you and the work you just did.

CHAPTER EIGHT

I'M AN ADULT NOW

Take a deep breath and relax. This next chapter is not as emotional as Chapter Seven. By the way, did you do the exercise? It's important for this chapter.

Now that you have done the work of letting go of the Little Me, you can focus on your adult self and getting to know who the adult you really are. But we do need to talk about something first, we should just get this out of the way.

Let's talk about hide and seek. You pick someone to be the seeker, they're the one who is it, and then you have the person who hides. Simple game, right? Well, not so simple in the game of Little Me, I'm an adult now. There are going to be times when Little Me is going to try to sneak back in and try to do it very slyly. So, for now you need to have your seeking on high alert. Pay attention to your feelings that come up in you and where they're coming from. Are they coming from a place of truth in this present moment emotion, or from a place where Little Me is hiding again in you?

Let's say it is Little Me, and you catch her, you need to let her go again. Simply say, "I see you, caught you, you cannot hide in me any longer. I love you, but you have to go. You may find yourself at first saying this a few times a day. Then it will lessen to maybe a few times a week, to just a couple times a month. Then hardly at all. Okay, that's all on that.

Now that you can be present in the current adult you, you can finally see yourself and all that you are. By the way, you're pretty amazing. I have been on this journey with you and feel like you are just an incredible person.

So, let's get sticky note happy for the next month. Every day I want you to write five positive words about yourself, just one word on each sticky note, whatever color you choose. Then you are going to post these notes throughout your home where you can see them every day. If we are going off of a thirty-day month, then at the end of the month you will have one hundred and fifty sticky notes all over your walls, bathroom mirrors, lamp shades, picture frames. Wherever you choose to put them.

Okay, you don't want sicky notes all over your house? I understand. But it's only thirty days of a life you already spent lost, so why not have fun with this exercise as you are discovering more about the adult you. If I guaranteed you at the end of thirty days you would hit the lotto, but you have to have one hundred and fifty sticky notes all over your home, you would do it without thinking! Here it is; you are going to hit the lotto. Your own version of the lotto. You are going to feel like a million bucks if you follow all the steps we have been journeying on together in this book.

Just think – there will be one hundred and fifty positive things about you. Wow! See, I told you that you're amazing! If anyone comes over and they ask, "Why do you have all these notes everywhere?" stand tall and proud and tell them, *"Because I'm that awesome!* Read them you will see how amazing I really am. I am one hundred and fifty fantastic words. Oh yeah, I *rock*!"

Every day you will walk in your home, reading notes about the greatness that is you. I know this may be uncomfortable for you to read and to say positive words about yourself. Do it anyway. Step into being uncomfortable – this is your growth time. You will learn to like reading, hearing, and saying good things about yourself. We all secretly love hearing good things about ourselves. I do! And I now I have no problem saying that out loud. *I love hearing good things about myself!* See? I told you I like it.

I hope at this point you really see your value, your importance, and how much you matter. Remember, you were created with great intention. Start living intentionally with complete love first for yourself. Your new adult self wants a relationship with you – one where you can go on walks with yourself, enjoying yourself. Basically, what I am saying is have a love affair with yourself, be in love with you. You will shine so bright people will be attracted to your light, your love.

Then guess who will show up? The partner you have longed for all this time. Your dream come true love, and why? Because you loved yourself first – so you attracted someone who would completely love you.

Hey, by the way, you're pretty fun! Okay, yes, we have gone through some big emotions, but still you are fun. So, don't forget as you're an adult to laugh like a child, be silly like a child. Not the Little Me child who was hurt, but a happy childlike attitude. Just have fun in your life, let go and enjoy the ride, it's your time to have fun. To love, live, and to laugh. Go for it all, you have nothing to lose, but everything to gain, my friend. Welcome to what your new adult self looks like.

Here's the rest of the story from the anonymous person from Chapter Four: "I am that strong woman that my mother wanted me to be, except full of love and kindness, and I can now see her love for me. God gave me a vision of her love that she could never show me. Then came a young man, the greatest man I have ever known and will ever know. He loved me more than life itself. He gave this strong, loving woman more meaning. We built together a beautiful, strong, family. I have come to realize that it is not what you were taught and learned in a little girl's body, it is what God gives you to form you into the adult person you were always meant to be. That is to know God's love for you. I now appreciate and grow with the hard times, and I cherish the good times."

And here's the rest of the story by Halee Koberlein from Chapter Five: "I have to say, I was headed down a bad path due to my loss of innocence. Then I had a beautiful baby girl, who changed my life forever. I now am a very successful hair dresser and have a home I love to live in. I have forgiven both my mother and father and have a close relationship with both of them. My sisters and I are all close, and I am so thankful for my family. Yes, my life is so good. I am very happy and living a stable life that is full of joy."

And finally, the rest of the story from Chapter Six: "I woke up one morning and realized I was turning into my mother. I knew I never wanted to be a victim and for sure did not want to put my family through this pain. So, I decided to free myself from that pain. I did the hard work in releasing Little Me. I have such a happy, fulfilled life where I don't complain and do not let people in my life mistreat me any longer. I'm not a victim; I'm an overcomer."

As for me? My ex-husband and I are now friends. It took hard work for each of us. Work on ourselves and work on forgiving each other. With forgiveness, all things are possible, because through forgiveness is where you heal.

I am still very good friends with the woman I dated for nine months. She is actually good friends with my husband and myself. With love and acceptance is where beauty and magic happen.

I was able to write this book because I pushed through my past pain and hurts and made it to the other side, where life is full of joy and magic. Yes, I still have times when Little me plays hide and seek. But I find her a lot faster now and tell her I love her, but she has to go. My life is not perfect, but I sure do love all of my life, even imperfections where I have to have more growing time. It's all beautiful. It's all a part of me transcending.

CHAPTER NINE

OBSTACLES

We have come so far in a short period. Remember that just because you are doing the hard work of healing does not mean life will be perfect by any means. You are going to have your valleys and your mountain tops. It's very important to not give up and fall into old patterns when you're in the valley. You really should be growing always in life. When you stop transcending, you become stagnant and this will lead you to nowhere.

Here is a metaphor: after winter, a river is in full rushing flow. It is in full force, flowing and rushing with speed. It knows its intention and where it's flowing to. It flows with certainty. Now, after months go by and the end of summer is nearing, the river starts to slow down. This river keeps slowing down, till it has no more flow. It has stopped. Moss is starting to form on this riverbed and on the rocks in the river. Bugs start hovering over this once-flowing river. It's just stagnant.

This can be what we become like if we do not keep our mind, body, and soul in check. If we give up and give into life's hardship we will most certainly stop growing and moving forward in our life. The valleys grow you, and the mountains bring you reprieve.

Don't settle in with complacency so that old behaviors try to creep back in. I want you to imagine yourself on an obstacle course. Every day you are weaving in and out of life's challenges, going up and down hills, making quick lefts, making quick rights. You will come up against something in this obstacle course that will put you to the test, that will make you doubt yourself and all that you are becoming. When that happens, I want you to get out sticky notes again. But this time, you are going to write three each day for one week (let's say a five-day work week) so that would be fifteen sticky notes. Write a sentence on three sticky notes about the good things that have come into your life. Read them. If the next week you are still feeling like you are in the valley, do this again, but use a different sentence. Stay in movement. It's okay to get sad, angry, or tired. Just stay in movement.

So, remember the note I had you write in Chapter Six? Well, I would like you to open this note and read what you wrote. Remember that this is truly your desire, and your desire is all a part of you and where you will be headed in your shifting. Take this note wherever you go; put it in your wallet, purse, glove box of your car. Just have it with you. When you start to doubt yourself, or have self-critical chatter, remember this is your path, your desire is coming into fruition and you love who you are becoming, and I want you to get the note out and read it, allowing this to be your reminder of what is your truth and that you are on your right path.

Stay proactive in your self-care. Remember that you have a relationship with yourself. So, treat yourself with love and compassion, be understanding with yourself, but do not make unhealthy excuses.

Take care of your vessel, eat healthy foods that nourish your body, go on walks or runs, go to the gym. Yoga is a great one for mind, body, and soul. Stay in self-care with self-love. Remember you are never alone in this life. Life can be a roller coaster, but since you're on it, make it fun! Don't grip so tight in fear; put your hands up and enjoy the ride. Try not to make things more complicated than they are. Just trust yourself. Use the tools you have been taught and you will be fine. You will be better than fine. You will *soar*.

CHAPTER TEN

CONCLUSION

Looks like it's time to wrap this up! I want to tell you how proud I am of you for picking up this book and taking this journey into understanding relationships and you, all of you from the Little You to the adult you. I think we have covered a lot here and that you now have so much more knowledge to take with you.

Now that you have really learned how and why it's so important to love yourself and to cherish who you are, I know that you will find that perfect relationship for you. The person of your dreams has been being molded for you, just as you have been for them. The time is drawing near for the two of you to finally join together. You just had to get prepared for one another.

My hope for you is that you always love yourself first. That you know your value. You can be all that you desire to be. It's all here for you. I hope you see the strength you have and the ability you have to use that strength for your greater good. May you see the world through the eyes of love for you are love. With love you can conquer all things. I hope you will always show grace to yourself and to others in your life. May you have love and acceptance in your heart for you and for others. I hope you show forgiveness for yourself and for others as well. I hope you will journey through life with you partner in great wonder and peace of the beautiful life you will be living. May you and your new love have great adventures, explore new avenues. Most of all, I wish you complete happiness in all that you do and all that you are.

Thank you so much for entrusting me with your journey. It was my pleasure to be here with you. Sending you all the love the Universe can give you. Don't forget to look up, the stars are shinning for you!

ACKNOWLEDGMENTS

Thank you, Author Incubator, for your fantastic program you have created in teaching the process of writing a book. For all the helpful advisors and for sure my amazing editor for all the time spent in working with me on my book.

Angela Lauria and her incredible wealth of knowledge. Your formulated program is one that is understandable and simple. Thank you for your beautiful heart you show to us all in your gift that you bring to the Universe.

Danette May: 2014 Your Time to Shine. A game changer for me.

Leslie Greey: You inspired me to write this book, thank you for showing up so bright.

I have so much gratitude to God, "My Source," for giving me the will and the strength to be the woman

I am today. To my spirit guides and God, I thank you so much for being the guides that guided my hands in the making of this book. For all your words of wisdom and encouragement along this journey. Thank you for always guiding me on the path of love and enlightenment.

I have learned that it is so important to appreciate yourself, so thank you to myself. Thank you for being present in your life, for taking steps in your life to make a difference in your life for yourself. Thank you, Self, for showing up for yourself by writing this book.

I would like to give such a big thank you to my awesome, wonderful husband for all his love, kindness, and support, and yes for sure patience as I journeyed in writing this book. Your unshakable love for me gave me the endurance to complete the book I started.

A big shout out *Thank You!* to my precious son, Robert, for cheering me on. For being such a support to me as your mother and friend. For your amazing wisdom and knowledge you brought to me in the process of this book.

My sweet, dear sister Wendy, thank you for being

an everyday ear for me to talk to, for all our deep conversations, and for being a confident. A sister can truly be your best friend.

Dear Dad and Mom, thank you for showing up for me the best you could for who you were at the time. I would never trade you for any other parents in the world. Thank you for helping in molding me into the enlightened women that I am today, for truly teaching me the gift of healing and forgiveness.

To my beautiful girlfriend Sherrie, you are with me every day you see all of me. The Good, Bad and the Ugly. Okay: and the beautiful. You are such an encourager. Thank you for picking up the slack when I couldn't, for just being there whenever I yelled "Sherrie!" Ha! You're the best and a huge blessing.

To my ex-husband. Thank you for working with me on mending our broken relationship, for helping us recreate a new kind of relationship with each other. Without my experience in our relationship, I would have never had the growth in understanding a deeper depth of relationships. I'm so thankful we have healed in our relationship and have a kind friendship with each other.

Last but for sure not least, I would like to take this time to tell you, the reader, how much I appreciate you for showing up for yourself by buying this book to help enlighten you on having that relationship you have always dreamed of. You are a superhero, your very own superhero. Thank you so much.

To my anonymous writers and to Halee Koberlein for sharing a part of your stories in my book, each so touching and heartfelt.

I appreciate and have so much love for each of you.

ABOUT THE AUTHOR

Colleen Traci is an intuitive Soul Guide who works in helping individuals heal from past traumas. She has been working with clients officially for the past five years, but has really been doing this work for twenty. Colleen has been working with clients one-on-one, in group sessions, and on healing retreats. Colleen uses her love and light to guide her in her practice. She discovered she had a unique way of reaching matters of the heart through her own journey with relationships. During this time, Colleen dove deep into studies on relationships to expand her level of gifting and knowledge into one.

Not only does Colleen work in healing the human psyche, but she also works with wildlife in their healing from human encroachment. It is Colleen's goal to bring love and light and healing to all different forms in our Universe with spiritual connection and dedication.

It is Colleen's honor and privilege to be able to share her light and love with so many people on their journey to healing. She knows she has been given a gift of light working to share with our Universe, and with this knowledge, Colleen feels a deep responsibility to make sure that she is doing her part to serve humanity.

ABOUT
DIFFERENCE PRESS

Difference Press offers entrepreneurs, including life coaches, healers, consultants, and community leaders, a comprehensive solution to get their books written, published, and promoted. A boutique-style alternative to self-publishing, Difference Press boasts a fair and easy-to-understand profit structure, low-priced author copies, and author-friendly contract terms. Its founder, Dr. Angela Lauria, has been bringing to life the literary ventures of hundreds of authors-in-transformation since 1994.

LET'S MAKE A DIFFERENCE WITH YOUR BOOK

You've seen other people make a difference with a book. Now it's your turn. If you are ready to stop watching and start taking massive action, reach out.

"Yes, I'm ready!"

In a market where hundreds of thousands books are published every year and are never heard from again, all participants of The Author Incubator have bestsellers that are actively changing lives and making a difference.

"In two years we've created over 250 bestselling books in a row, 90% from first-time authors." We do this by selecting the highest quality and highest potential applicants for our future programs.

Our program doesn't just teach you how to write a book—our team of coaches, developmental editors, copy editors, art directors, and marketing experts incubate you from book idea to published bestseller, ensuring that the book you create can actually make a difference in the world. Then we give you the training you need to use your book to make the difference you want to make in the world, or to create a business out of serving your readers. If you have life-or world-changing ideas or services, a servant's heart, and the willingness to do what it REALLY takes to make a difference in the world with your book, go to http://theauthorincubator.com/apply/ to complete an application for the program today.

OTHER BOOKS BY DIFFERENCE PRESS

Secrets of the Zen Business Warrior: 7 Steps to Grow Your Business, Feel Excited, and Stay Motivated

by Lina Betancur

Rewrite Your Life Without Dermatographia: The All-Natural Solution to Managing Hive-like Welts and Severe Itching

by Sandra Graneau

Sick of Being Sick: The Woman's Holistic Guide to Conquering Chronic Illness

by Brenda Walding

Move Freely: Get Your Life Back After Injury

by Helen Blake

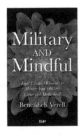

Military and Mindful: Eight Essential Elements to Manage Your Military Career and Motherhood

by Benefsheh Verell

THANK YOU!

As an offer for buying this book, I would like to give you a *free* half-hour session with me. Just go to my website at **ColleenTraci.com** and click Book A Session. This will give you the opportunity to work one-on-one with me through Zoom or a phone call, or even in person. Thank you for reading my book and taking this journey with me.